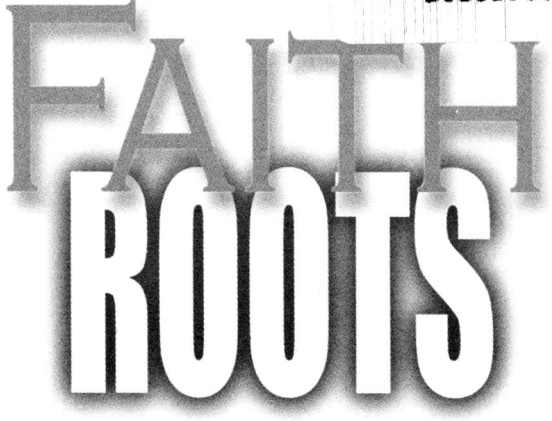

FAITH ROOTS

Mark Finley
and Steven Mosley

Pacific Press® Publishing Association
Nampa, Idaho
Oshawa, Ontario, Canada
www.pacificpress.com

Cover design by Fred Knopper
Cover photo by Photodisc

Additional copies of this book are available by
calling toll free 1-800-765-6955 or visiting
http://www.adventistbookcenter.com.

ISBN: 0-8163-1996-0

03 04 05 06 07 • 5 4 3 2 1

Contents

The Secret of Resilience 5

Too Fast for Faith? 15

How Can I Feel Safe? 25

Does God Really Make a Difference? 35

How Many Redeemers? 44

Is There a Remnant? 53

The Secret of Resilience

Some kids from abusive homes will struggle all their lives just to function normally. Other kids from the same kinds of homes will enjoy great success.

What makes the difference?

Science is beginning to uncover the secret of resilience. For years we've been hearing about how our genes and our environment determine our destiny. Psychologists have focused on all the ways in which human beings are damaged. Social scientists have determined risk factors—the things that put children and families at risk. We've heard a lot on the news about violent neighborhoods, substandard education, poverty, neglectful or abusive parents. These are the factors that drive kids to crime or to drugs or to a life of broken relationships.

But then came a landmark study on the island of Kauai of 700 infants born in 1955. Many of these were "at risk" kids. They were headed for trouble. But researchers followed their development for four decades. And they discovered that a lot of kids don't fit the script. Many individuals from the worst environments just aren't failing in life as they're "supposed" to. They grow up to be healthy, productive adults. Lots of people overcome intense stress and adversity.

Today, more and more researchers are zeroing in on the "protective factors" that enable individuals to bounce back. There's a new wind blowing through the field of psychology. Instead of trying to explain human behavior in terms of uncontrollable factors, psychologists are uncovering ways in which people achieve a better life.

Well, what have they come up with? All of us would like to be more resilient. We'd like to thrive in adversity. So what's the secret? What is it that makes some "at risk" individuals overcome the odds?

Dr. Albert Bandura, a Stanford University professor and one of the pioneers in this new field, has identified the key ingredient in resilience. He calls it "self-efficacy"—the belief that action will produce results.

Now that may not sound very startling. Doesn't everyone believe that actions will produce results? The answer is, No. Victims don't. People who are overwhelmed by adversity don't. People who can't get beyond a bad environment don't. Some individuals come to believe that what they do won't really make a difference. They feel helpless. They just go with the flow. They don't realize that these very assumptions keep them trapped in bad circumstances. That's what it really boils down to.

Self-efficacy is the conviction that I can change things. It's the assumption that I am responsible for my life. As Dr. Bandura puts it: "People have the power to influence what they do and to make things happen."

In recent years, we've learned about the harmful effects of stress on the immune system. Stress breaks the body down, we've been told. But did you know there is also a body of research that shows that stress, *coupled with a belief that a problem can be overcome,* actually *strengthens* the immune system. Same stress, different attitudes—totally different physical impact.

Two major studies looked at African-American and Hispanic adolescents in Chicago and analyzed the key difference between those who showed resilience and those who didn't. What made the difference? "A stronger cognitive motivational pattern." In plain English, "a more positive attitude." The resilient teens believed they could change their environment.

Did you know that this same essential quality, this same belief, is highlighted in the New Testament? Yes, long before these psychological studies Christ and His apostles understood what resilience is really about. And they shed a very special light on the subject. Paul was a man who knew plenty about adversity. Listen to his great affirmation: "I can do all things through Christ who strengthens me" (Philippians 4:13).

Now that's self-efficacy! That's confidence! Paul didn't just believe that his actions would produce positive results. He believed that he could do "all things." But that confidence was firmly grounded in his faith in Christ. Christ enabled him to do all things. Christ strengthened him to meet such challenges as imprisonment and shipwreck—with cheerful resilience.

In the New Testament, it's faith that enables us to keep believing that our actions will produce positive results—even in the worst of circumstances. Faith is the key ingredient in resilience. Listen to Jesus' great affirmation about faith: "I tell you the truth, if you have faith as small as a mustard seed, you can say to this mountain, 'Move from here to there' and it will move. Nothing will be impossible for you" (Matthew 17:20, 21, NIV).

Faith enables us to move mountains. That's the good news Christ brings us. With faith, nothing is impossible. Faith is a shield that protects us from the flaming arrows of the enemy. Faith enables us to overcome the world. Faith keeps us safe. Yes, faith in God is the ultimate protective factor. It's the surest path to resilience.

Today, research is beginning to demonstrate precisely that fact. Here's one study published by Cambridge University Press. A sociologist studied children from all kinds of backgrounds and communities. And then he zeroed in on the most resilient children among them. What did they have in common? According to the report, the common factor was: "Religious beliefs that provided stability and meaning to their lives, especially in times of hardship."

Dr. Albert Bandura looked at families who best helped their children overcome obstacles and challenges in their environments. One of the things that stood out was this: Successful families developed links with local churches and other social organizations that gave their kids positive role models. These were parents, Bandura reports, who didn't let their dismal environment defeat them. They created social ties that helped protect their kids against the dangers in their world.

The same holds true of schools. Researchers discovered that certain schools helped "at risk" kids much more than others. Why? Teachers in those schools tended to believe that their students had the capacity for resilience. They believed that individuals can change—and even transform—their lives. They had high expectations.

Interesting, isn't it? People who believed they would find resilience actually developed it. People who believed their students could accomplish more, enabled them to do just that. Yes, even kids from impoverished homes. Yes, even kids from violent neighborhoods. Yes, even kids with drug-addicted parents.

These kids found someone who believed in them. And they latched on to that. They formed nurturing relationships with better role models. They responded to those high expectations.

Do you realize that this is exactly what can happen in a community of faith? This is why Christ founded His church. It can be a gold mine of resilience.

Listen to how the writer of Hebrews describes relationships in Christ's body, the church: "Let us draw near to God with a sincere heart in full assurance of faith. . . . And let us consider how we may spur one another on toward love and good deeds. Let us not give up meeting together . . . but let us encourage one another." (Hebrews 10:22, 24, 25, NIV).

Drawing near to God helps us draw near to one another. The assurance of faith helps us assure others. Knowing that we can do all things in Christ helps us "spur one another on toward love and good deeds." God's encouragement enables us to encourage others. This is what a community of faith can do. It produces resilience.

Dr. Wendy Haight conducted a four-year study of African-American children in Salt Lake City, Utah. These were children who regularly experienced isolation and discrimination. But at the First Baptist Church they attended, these kids experienced something very different. Dr. Haight carefully documented the ways in which Sunday School teachers developed faith in these children.

And what were the results? They developed a sense of belonging. They developed a healthy self-esteem. They identified with a gospel message of love and hope and equality. And they were able to rise above hatred. They were able to rise above the low expectations of many teachers in their city. Dr. Haight demonstrated that the experience of developing faith in church made these kids significantly more resilient.

Researchers have found that positive group experiences help people become more resilient in another way as well. Besides believing in people, besides having high expectations, positive groups also provide opportunities for individuals to participate, to get involved. That's true in school. If kids can find responsible roles to fulfill in their schools, they tend to develop resilient traits.

And meaningful participation is exactly what a community of faith offers. There's a beautiful picture in the New Testament of what the church really is. In 1 Corinthians 12, Paul compares the church to a body made up of many different members. Each member of the body has a vital role to play. Where would the body be without eyes to see? Where would the body be without feet to walk? Where would the body be without ears to hear?

Similarly, each member of Christ's body, each member of a church, has a spiritual gift, some ability to contribute. And every gift is vital to the function of the whole body. Some are teachers. Some are scholars. Some are good listeners. Some have the gift of hospitality. But everyone can participate meaningfully—according to their gifts. That's what a community of faith offers.

And, as we know now, that's one of the ways to develop resilience. So, if you want to bounce back, get involved in a local congregation. If you want to be an overcomer, find a way to participate.

That's part of what Dr. Haight demonstrated in her study of children in Salt Lake City. Those kids didn't just come to church and sit idly in the pew; they got very involved in the stories told, very involved in the discussions of what faith means.

A community of faith does make a profound difference. The Bible clearly shows us that faith is the best way to self-efficacy. Faith is the foundation of resilience. Faith in God. Faith in what Christ can do for you. Faith invested in other people. Faith expressed in a community.

James had some very interesting comments on faith:

> What does it profit, my brethren, if someone says he has faith but does not have works? Can faith save him? If a brother or sister is naked and destitute of daily food, and one of you says to them, "Depart in peace, be warmed and filled," but you do not give them the things which are needed for the body, what does it profit? Thus also faith by itself, if it does not have works, is dead (James 2:14-17).

Many scholars see these words as part of a theological debate. For some, they're proof texts used to define saving faith precisely. For others they're a problem that must be reconciled with justification by faith.

But I believe these words have great relevance—just as they are—when it comes to practical living, when it comes to resilience. James's great burden is to show that genuine faith, living faith, is not something passive. It doesn't replace action. It inspires action. It expresses itself through action.

And that, again, is the crucial element in resilience—believing that actions produce results. The person who claims to have faith but doesn't do anything for a destitute friend is really saying, "I can't help; my contribution won't make a difference."

Real faith, James insists, is believing that you must act because your actions make a difference. They make a difference because God is at work in us. They make a difference because God makes all things possible through faith.

James pointed back to the father of faith, Abraham, as an example of this healthy kind of belief. This was the Abraham who acted in response to God's command. The patriarch who followed God out of Chaldea into a great adventure. The man who believed God and had it counted as righteousness. The man who became the father of a great nation.

"Do you see that faith was working together with his works, and by works faith was made perfect?" (James 2:22).

The life of faith and the active life aren't on opposite ends of the spectrum. They function best together. Our faith gives our actions great potential. And it's these actions, in turn, which intensify our faith. Faith grows deeper as it is expressed. That, my friends, is the ultimate secret of resilience.

God has a great plan for you to develop resilience. He can make you an overcomer. He can help you to prosper in times of adversity. He can strengthen you on the inside. He can enable you to do all things.

Your environment may be forbidding. You may have obstacles all around you. You may come from a dysfunctional family. You may have handicaps or addictions.

But God is bigger than all that.

Are you feeling helpless? God is bigger than your habit.

Are people putting you down? God believes in you much more.

Have you been labeled a loser? God has high expectations.

Do you feel abandoned? God gave up everything to claim you as His own.

You just can't have a better Person on your side. So isn't it time to respond with a little faith? Isn't it time to respond with whatever faith you can muster?

Tell God, "Here I am. I'm willing to act. I'm willing to take responsibility. I'm willing to make better choices. I'm willing because You make good things happen. You magnify the results."

Tell God, "Here I am." He will set your feet surely on the road to resilience.

Too Fast for Faith?

Somebody pressed "Fast Forward." Have you noticed? Society is on hyper-drive. Messages hit us at a relentless pace—cell phones, faxes, pagers, overnight letters, and emails. And we have to respond in kind just to keep up. We find ourselves surfing through one hundred cable options or clicking through countless Web sites. There's so much competition, so much pressure to keep up.

In this kind of world, people are beginning to wonder: Are we traveling too fast for faith? Can spiritual values keep up? Do the old guidelines still make sense?

In Los Angeles, near where I live, commuters have taken to solving traffic disputes with handguns. Freeway etiquette literally can be a life-or-death issue! In suburbs across the country, designer drugs are getting into junior high schools. Hard-core porn is no longer confined to an alley on the other side of town. Now, it's in our homes—at a Web site just a few mouse clicks away from the kids.

At the same time, international terrorist groups are slamming planes into buildings and turning deadly biological viruses into weapons of mass destruction. Threats come at us on a much bigger scale today—as the twenty-four-hour global news networks constantly show us. One little computer virus can bring an entire economy to a standstill. The guy wandering around the airport could have a nuclear device in his backpack.

How do we live one day at a time—in the middle of a storm? How are we to grow healthy families? How are we to find a measure of peace?

Well, in the New Testament, we find a word to the wise that is offered as the antidote to stress and anxiety. It's an idea that the apostles repeat over and over—live by faith.

Faith stands out as the quality the New Testament talks about the most. The apostles centered their gospel around it. Jesus Christ kept pointing the lame, the blind, the proud, and the broken to it as their only hope. Here are just a few of the New Testament's 483 references to faith and belief:

- "The just shall live by faith" (Romans 1:17).
- "We walk by faith, not by sight" (2 Corinthians 5:7).
- "I live by faith in the Son of God" (Galatians 2:20).
- "Faith is the substance of things hoped for, the evidence of things not seen" (Hebrews 11:1).

But the question is, do the old guidelines still work? Does faith hold up in the middle of a storm? On the one hand we're supposed to trust, to believe that we're safe in God's hand. But what if our environment isn't so hospitable? What if it's downright dangerous? Does faith mean we have to pretend that the world around us is safer than it really is? Is living by faith just whistling in the dark?

Today, the world tells us to live by our wits. That seems to make sense in the fast-track world of high-tech. We're told to live by the laws of science. We're told to live defensively. But live by faith? That may have worked in a time when people tended sheep by still waters and green pastures. Today, life whizzes by us at the speed of Internet access. We can fall behind just by blinking. How are we supposed to keep our eyes on the unseen and not on the things of this world?

Well, let's get a feel for what the New Testament writers actually meant when they said to live by faith. They describe faith as something that can greatly expand our abilities. They claim it can fill us up "with all the fullness of God" (Ephesians 3:19). They claim it can move mountains.

Here's how. The apostle Paul gives us the first clue. "We have believed in Christ Jesus, that we might be justified by faith in Christ and not by the works of the law; for by the works of the law no flesh shall be justified" (Galatians 2:16). To be justified by faith means that you are accepted, declared righteous by faith. It boils down to this: You *accept* God's love instead of trying to *earn* it.

Now, that truth has a very practical application for daily life. What does living by faith mean? First of all, faith is about stopping. We can accomplish more by being still.

A friend of mine discovered this truth one muggy afternoon underneath his van. Steve just couldn't get the oil filter off. It wouldn't budge. He spent a half hour trying to wrench it off. Giving up in a fury, he started to lift the driver's seat so he could pour four quarts of clean oil into the engine underneath. But part of the seat jammed against an arm rest. He could lift it only a couple of inches. He needed to open the driver's door in order to get the seat up. But the door on the driver's side was stuck shut; the electronic lock just wouldn't disengage. Now Steve got *really* mad! He pushed every button in sight. Nothing happened.

His predicament hit him. He couldn't lift the seat to get oil in because the door wouldn't open. But, he couldn't go get it fixed because there was no oil in the van! And he couldn't get oil in the van because . . .

That's when Steve really lost it. Stomping into the garage, he grabbed a screwdriver and a pair of pliers and began yanking and twisting on the driver's door lock. He abused that stubborn lock for a long time.

Finally, exhausted, he slumped back in the passenger seat. He began feeling a little embarrassed about his temper tantrum and decided to pray about the problem. He stopped. He took a deep breath. He looked God's way and said, "Please help me not to be consumed by this. Help me put it in Your hands."

Well, after saying "Amen," he glanced over at the driver's door. For some reason, he noticed the door handle, tucked away in the upholstery. Steve thought he'd yanked on it, along with everything else in reach. But he leaned over anyway and pulled it back. *Click.* That sharp, clean sound struck him like the ringing of a cathedral bell. The door swung open effortlessly.

You know, Steve spent quite a bit of that afternoon thrashing against the machine. He shrank into a little ball of rage. But then he remembered faith. He stopped. He prayed. And faith made something more out of him. He could get out of himself. He became a calmer, saner person capable of trying something else.

Faith calms us. That's the first way it enables us to accomplish much more. Sometimes we scream, "There's not enough of me to go around!" We use up a lot of energy fighting an immovable object. But faith helps us stop. We relax a bit, remembering God's care for the lilies of the field and the birds of the air.

And that brings us to the second way faith works to enable us to accomplish more. Faith connects us to a God who has an infinite number of solutions. Faith is about focusing our attention on those solutions.

When two blind men by a Galilean road accosted Jesus, He got them to focus on His power. He asked them, "Do you believe that I am able to do this?" (Matthew 9:28). They did believe, and Jesus was able to heal them.

On another occasion, a leper approached Jesus and said, "If You are willing, You can make me clean" (Matthew 8:2). The Master rewarded his faith immediately and cleansed him of his disease.

Jesus wanted people to affirm the fact that He could meet their needs. He wanted people looking not at how big, or how small, their faith was, but at how big God is.

Let me tell you about how an Arkansas farm boy discovered the bigness of God.

One blustery, rainy day, Raymond huddled with his family in the cellar. He was listening to a tornado tear through Texarkana. It was littering its wake with telephone poles, livestock, and post offices. Little Raymond's eyes were glued to the rattling cellar door. He thought any second the storm would plunge in and drag him away.

The tornado passed, however. The homestead was repaired, and life resumed its slow pace. But for Raymond, the terror remained. He never felt safe. The earth itself had exposed him to terrible danger. Every darkening of the sky petrified him. Every gust of wind through the treetops froze the boy's pulse. He could hardly function. Raymond thought the fear would never leave him.

But one Sunday, a visiting minister came to Raymond's white-frame church. He spoke about the power of faith and prayer. He insisted that God is big enough to meet our smallest and greatest needs.

Raymond decided to try it out. That afternoon, he slipped off into the woods by himself. Looking into the sky, he told God he was awfully tired of this fear. "Would You, please, Sir, mind taking it away?" Raymond asked. Then he went back to plowing the cornfield.

A few days later, Raymond realized he hadn't felt afraid since his prayer in the woods. A few gray clouds had gone by, the wind had picked up a couple of times, but that acid fear in his stomach was gone. Apparently, God had simply dissolved it.

Some years later, Raymond found himself on a navy ship in the middle of the Pacific. A fierce storm came up and quickly lashed the sea into a frenzy. Fifty-foot waves exploded against his troop carrier. The ship swayed and pitched so violently that everyone fled below deck. Only a few officers remained on the bridge trying to hold the ship on course.

Everyone fled, that is, except Raymond. He stood there, soaked with spray, clinging tightly to an upper-deck railing. This sailor found himself enjoying the storm immensely. He'd been cramped for so long aboard ship. Now his youthful energies seemed to shout with the forces clashing from horizon to horizon. It was exhilarating. Raymond actually celebrated God's majesty and omnipotence out there in the storm. He felt awed and humbled before the vast drama around him.

Faith expands us—in the middle of a storm. Faith enables us to do just fine—in the middle of a storm. Why? Because faith connects us to a God who is bigger than a heaving ocean. It connects us to a God of infinite solutions and boundless possibilities.

Friends, we're traveling too fast *not* to have faith! We need to connect with the God who moves at the speed of light, the God who transcends time and space. We need faith to keep up!

Faith isn't just for people who can't make it on their own. Faith isn't just for individuals whose lives are falling apart. Yes, of course, faith helps the weak. We all have weaknesses. But faith also energizes the able-bodied. Faith is what enables us to accomplish far more than what is humanly possible.

In fact, the author of Hebrews presents faith as the distinguishing mark of heroes. Hebrews 11 spotlights a parade of individuals down through history who accomplished great feats by faith. They built an ark to save life on the planet. They created nations in hostile environments. They blessed their descendants for generations to come. They led slaves to freedom. They conquered impregnable fortresses. Listen to this inspiring summary:

> And what more shall I say? For the time would fail me to tell of Gideon and Barak and Samson and Jephthah, also of David and Samuel and the prophets: who through faith subdued kingdoms, worked righteousness, obtained promises, stopped the mouths of lions, quenched the violence of fire, escaped the edge of the sword, out of weakness were made strong, became valiant in battle, turned to flight the armies of the aliens (Hebrews 11:32-34).

That's what faith enables us to do. It stretches us from the inside out. Faith enables us to keep up with the God of light.

One of the most fascinating individuals I've ever met is a Cuban pastor named Humberto Noble Alexander. I got to know him after his release from twenty years of confinement in one of Castro's prisons. What struck me most about this man, however, was how cheery and good-humored he seemed. And I learned something that amazed me. This cheery man had baptized 200 fellow inmates into the Lord Jesus Christ—right under the noses of the guards!

How did this happen? I couldn't imagine. Religious practice of any kind was forbidden in this prison.

Well, Humberto usually managed to do it during the noon meal when two lines of prisoners were crowded around a long trough of water where they washed up. He'd lower the baptismal candidate into the water in the name of the Father, Son, and Holy Spirit, and then slip back into line.

Now, more often than not, the authorities found out about the secret baptism. But do you know what Humberto would say about that? He'd say, "That's OK; he was already baptized."

Would Pastor Humberto be beaten? Yes, probably. Would Pastor Humberto be brutalized? Yes, probably. But what mattered to him was that an individual had already embarked on a new journey of faith.

Humberto Noble Alexander was sustained for two decades by a living faith in his Lord Jesus Christ. He didn't just cope by faith; he accomplished great things by faith. His faith wasn't a crutch; it was a weapon he wielded to great effect against overwhelming obstacles.

The writer of Hebrews celebrates men and women "who out of weakness were made strong," people who "quenched the violence of fire" (Hebrews 11:34), people "of whom the world was not worthy" (verse 38).

Are we moving too fast for faith today? We're moving too fast *not* to have faith! Are you living by faith today? Or are you still trying to earn acceptance?

Are you trusting God today? Or are you trying to do it all on your own? You'll go so much farther with faith. And above all, you'll be moving in the right direction.

You just can't go wrong fixing your eyes on Jesus. I invite you to take that step of faith right now. It doesn't matter what baggage you may bring with you. It doesn't matter what troubles are dragging you down. God is big enough. Faith is the way God gives you leverage to overcome.

So, please bring whatever trust you have and invest it in the living God. He will do wonders with whatever you bring to Him.

How Can I Feel Safe?

Ever since that terrible morning when the unthinkable exploded into view on our TV screens, we've been struggling with one all-important issue—security. It's as if, in the wreckage of the World Trade Center towers, the ground has been taken out from under all of us.

- We feel it in an airline jet flying overhead.
- We feel it when gazing up at a tall building.
- We feel it at any large, public event.
- We feel it when we pass a nuclear power plant or a government building.

Fear hits us in places and at times it never did before. And we're all wondering: Can I ever feel safe again?

Frencesco, a New York City high-school teacher, won't go near a subway now unless he sees armed security guards posted there. Why? Because his wife, Rose, had just come up out of a station when she heard the horrible sound of a plane smashing into World Trade Center Tower Two.

Olivia watched the same tower collapse from several blocks away. Now, she can scarcely leave her home in New Jersey. She says, "I feel nervous in my own bedroom."

Those explosions in New York City and Washington D.C. have shaken us up. The ripple of fear has spread far beyond those cities and enveloped the whole country. Becky, in Roswell, Georgia, for example, has decided not to attend any more Atlanta Braves games. She explains, "There are crazy people out there."

"How can I feel safe?" That's the question on our minds. Terrorists could strike anywhere.

How do we counteract fear? Well, the first important thing we can do is to get the facts. Whenever tragedy strikes, and people feel confused and uncertain, do you know what always rushes in to fill the vacuum? Rumors of all kinds. Fear stimulates our imaginations. We heard about crop dusters supposedly flying where there are no crops, perhaps engaged in biological warfare. The Internet buzzed with a rumor about a "Klingerman virus," claimed to be on sponges sent to people in blue envelopes. We need to counter cold fear with hard facts.

Here is one of the most important facts: Even with all the attention given to terrorism, your chances of being killed in a terrorist attack are about the same as being killed by an iron safe falling on you from a fifth-floor window.

Now, I recognize that fact won't bring back those lost loved ones for thousands of grieving families. But it can give all of us some much-needed perspective. It makes sense to take precautions in certain situations.

It makes sense for the government to invest more in homeland defense.

But it doesn't make sense to keep looking over your shoulder all the time. It doesn't make sense to react in fear every time you see a young man of Middle Eastern descent pass you on the street. It doesn't make sense to keep looking up for the safe that might possibly drop on you from the fifth-floor window.

One of the great principles Jesus emphasized is that the truth sets us free. One of the main benefits of focusing on the truth is that it sets us free from fear.

The apostle Paul spotlights this point. Talking about how we can stand firm against the assaults of the enemy, he says, "Therefore take up the whole armor of God, that you may be able to withstand in the evil day, and having done all, to stand. Stand therefore, having girded your waist with truth" (Ephesians 6:13, 14).

How do we stand against fear? With the belt of truth buckled around our waist. That's good advice. That's God's advice.

So, first of all, get the facts, get some perspective. Don't let rumors or your imagination picture what the world around you is really like.

Facts are good, but we need more than facts. After all, fear is an emotion, a strong emotion. And anxiety performs a certain function in our lives. That's why it can keep going and going and going. A lot of us actually use anxiety as a way of trying to escape some greater pain. Anxiety becomes a kind of sacrifice we make to the uncertain future. We secretly hope that if we worry enough, all those bad things won't happen to us.

The problem is, the emotions we generate in the process are often more harmful than the bad things we fear. Prolonged worry and anxiety produce serious wear and tear on the body. We may think it's the threat of terror and disaster that's producing stress in our lives. But what's really hurting us is our own reaction to that perceived danger.

Terror, in other words, isn't just a problem *out there.* It's a problem *in here.*

So God gives us another great principle that can powerfully counteract fear. It's a message embodied in the command Jesus gave to an individual who'd been paralyzed for decades: "Rise, take up your bed and walk" (John 5:8).

For those who are paralyzed by fear, God says, "Get up and do something. Get up, and I'll perform a miracle."

In other words, we just can't remain passive in the face of fear. Don't just sit there and let anxiety inflate around you. Don't let it paralyze you.

Paul told his disciple Timothy, "God has not given us a spirit of fear, but of power and of love and of a sound mind" (2 Timothy 1:7). God wants us to respond to threats with His power, with energetic action, and self-discipline. He also wants us to reach out in love. Fear can either drive us into a shell or force us to expand our circle. The difference is whether we allow God's love to work through us.

Sometimes we just react, instead of act. Some people, after the September 11 attacks, rushed out to grab hold of something, anything, to make them feel more secure. They snapped up 400 Desert Storm gas masks, hoping that would save them in a chemical attack. They stockpiled bottled water. Some even hoarded drugs they thought would save them from the effects of biological warfare.

There are other things we can do to fight fear that make more sense. This is what counselors are suggesting, counselors who work with people who've been through a traumatic event:

- Get back to your usual routine as much and as soon as possible.
- Talk to people; talk about your feelings with others.
- Socialize in various ways. Invest time in other people. Help other people. Give someone a hug or an encouraging word.
- Everyday, tell your family that you love them.

These are some of the ways you can counteract fear with action—positive action. You don't have to remain passive in the face of fear. You don't have to be overwhelmed.

Now let me show you something else you can do that is probably the greatest antidote of all to fear. What we need more than anything else, in the face of terror and tragedy, is a sense of peace. I'd like to show you the world's greatest Peacemaker in action. He's the Source of a unique kind of peace that is stronger than all the sorrows of the world. And we need to get a clear picture of Him in our minds.

Jesus Christ was crossing the Sea of Galilee one afternoon with His disciples. It was a trip He'd taken many times with these fishermen who had become fishers of men.

But on this day, a storm came up suddenly and whipped the lake into a frenzy. Waves crashed over the boat. The fierce wind ripped their sail apart. It got so bad that these seasoned fishermen panicked; they were sure they'd all drown.

But Jesus stood up and put a hand against the mast. Facing into the fury of the wind, He calmly spoke three words, "Peace, be still" (Mark 4:39). And suddenly everything quieted down. The dark clouds overhead cleared. The wind died down. The lake flattened out.

The disciples sat there stunned, looking out at the glassy, blue water. Do you know what they were looking at? They were looking at a peace that surpasses comprehension. They were looking at peace in the midst of a storm. In amazement they looked at one another and said, "Who can this be, that even the wind and the sea obey Him!" (Mark 4:41).

Who could this be? Jesus is the One who holds the elements in His hands. The One who can transform the most perilous of situations. Jesus creates peace. And Jesus promises to bring peace to each one of us. He says, "These things I have spoken to you, that in Me you may have peace. In the world you will have tribulation; but be of good cheer, I have overcome the world" (John 16:33).

Scary things can happen in this world. Troubles will come our way. But Jesus has overcome all the evil in the world. He's overcome the chaos on the outside, and the chaos on the inside. He's stronger than anything that might threaten us. That's the reason He can bring us peace. It's not just a nice sentiment. There is great power behind Jesus Christ's peace. It's something we can claim in the most dangerous of circumstances.

On another afternoon, the townspeople of Gergesa discovered this peace that passes comprehension. It happened on the shore of the lake. They had come out to check on two lunatics who had been terrorizing their community for years. The Gergesenes hadn't been able to subdue them even with chains and shackles. And now, these two men had broken out again and tried to attack a stranger named Jesus.

The townspeople arrived on the scene and came up short. There were the two lunatics, sitting at the feet of Jesus, clothed and in their right minds. They were calmly talking with the Man. They had the light of peace in their eyes. This was impossible! These were men who were always gashing themselves with stones and shrieking half the night!

But there they sat, talking about how wonderful and brand new they felt. The Gergesenes stared at the evidence of an extraordinary Peacemaker. He had molded the total chaos in these two men's minds into reason and self-awareness.

You know, often our fears boil down to simply what we think about the most. What we habitually dwell on makes a big difference. Our success in dealing with fear will depend on which is bigger in our minds—the potential danger or Christ the Peacemaker. We can either fret over possible tragedies or concentrate on Christ's promises. We can worry about the threats out there or focus on the God who stands beside us.

Paul puts it this way in words of hope, encouragement, and peace: "Be anxious for nothing, but in everything by prayer and supplication, with thanksgiving, let your requests be made known to God; and the peace of God, which surpasses all understanding, will guard your hearts and minds through Christ Jesus" (Philippians 4:6, 7).

There you have it. That's the peace that surpasses all understanding. It comes from Christ. And it comes when we lay everything out to Him in prayer. It comes when we're honest with Him. It comes when we turn over our joys and sorrows to Him.

The prophet Isaiah highlights the same basic point: "You will keep him in perfect peace, whose mind is stayed on You, because he trusts in You" (Isaiah 26:3). Perfect peace comes from a mind that's focused on God. Perfect peace comes from concentrating on the One we can trust perfectly.

God can be the great constant in our lives—a peaceful, still spot for the ups and downs of circumstances. We may have had a bad week, but He has good plans for all eternity. We may feel intimidated by the threat of terror, but the Almighty crushes His adversaries in the dust.

We need to focus on the person of God Himself. That's the best way to cancel out all the negatives. He's bigger than our problems. He's better than our failures. He's more promising than our worries. He simply outweighs everything—if we get a close enough view to place Him in perspective.

Make no mistake, God does promise to stand beside us. The Hebrew psalmist discovered that long ago. He wrote: "I will say of the Lord, 'He is my refuge and my fortress; my God, in Him I will trust.' He shall cover you with His feathers, and under His wings you shall take refuge; His truth shall be your shield and buckler. You shall not be afraid of the terror by night, nor of the arrow that flies by day" (Psalm 91:2, 4, 5).

What a beautiful reassuring picture of our mighty Lord. We find refuge under His wings. His faithfulness is like a shield. He is the One who can neutralize "the terror of night."

Let's look at another positive statement of faith: "The Lord is my light and my salvation; whom shall I fear? The Lord is the strength of my life; of whom shall I be afraid?" (Psalm 27:1). Whom indeed should we fear, with the Lord at our side? Think about the picture of God that such verses give us. It will help so much if we look at the dangers in the world through the sheltering arms of the God who is our fortress, defense, refuge, and shield.

In the end, God has promised us throughout the history of the world that He will not leave us comfortless and that He will be with us in our trials and that evil will not stand. He has promised that good will overcome evil. I have faith in that. I believe that if we put our faith in God, He will not disappoint us.

We have a better world to look for. We can look up to God and know there's a better life after this. We have trials and troubles here, but one day there will be only peace. My faith is the only thing that helps me see through the difficult times in which we live today. I know God loves us, and I know He has a plan for us. When tragedies strike, it may be hard to see anything positive at all, but these things bring out the best in people, and they can help us to find God. Those who may not have seen His hand in their lives in the past, can be shown the only place to find peace.

How can you feel safe today? You can feel safe by keeping your eyes on grace, keeping your eyes on the Peacemaker, keeping your eyes on the Almighty God, who is our refuge in times of trouble.

I invite you today to bring your anxieties and fears to the One who understands you best. I invite you to tell Him what you're feeling. Tell Him all about it. He's big enough to take it all in. And then, please keep looking His way. Don't let threats out there set up camp in here. Don't let the dangers in the world block out the One who so loved the world.

I invite you to do that right now. Bring to Him your fear. Bring to Him your worry. Bring to Him your anxiety. Bring to Him everything that troubles you. Refocus your mind, not on your problems, not on your difficulties, not on the challenge, not on your heartache or sorrow. Refocus your mind on Jesus, the One who loves you, the One who cares for you, the One who knows all about your problems.

Does God Really Make a Difference?

Do you believe it's possible to get back to the roots of faith? Back to a time when it sprung up strong and tall as an oak tree?

Have you noticed what's been happening in the aftermath of attacks on national security, in America and elsewhere? People are reaching back to traditional beliefs. People are trying to find something solid to hang on to. People are trying to find roots for their faith.

Cynicism is out. Making light of allegiance and devotion doesn't make sense anymore. We realize we're in a deadly earnest struggle against the enemies of freedom and democracy. We're looking through the smoke toward a flag we hope is still standing.

That's where we are today. Needing to believe that right and truth will prevail. But needing, more than ever, some kind of solid ground for that faith.

Let's spend a few moments in this chapter looking for faith roots we can count on. Let's deal with some recent challenges that are keeping people from finding those roots. Maybe we can get back to a place where

35

things are more sure. Maybe we can find a place of peace in a world that won't quite stop shaking.

One big challenge people are facing today is this question: Does God really make a difference? Does He really change people? That's an important question. A solid faith—a faith with roots—has to be connected to a God who actually elevates us and makes us better.

Scandals in the church, terrible crimes seeping into the church, have caused people to question God. A while back, people in Boston were shocked to hear that perhaps up to seventy priests in the archdiocese had abused young people in their care. Catholics were appalled—priests molesting young children! In some instances, church leaders had failed to stop the perpetrators.

And then the scandal spread far beyond Boston. People of faith, in general, were deeply troubled. How could so many clergymen be doing such horrible things?

It's scandals such as these that make people wonder whether God really makes a difference. If those consecrated to His service, if those who've taken vows of celibacy, commit such crimes, what hope is there for the rest of us?

Something's very wrong if a church ends up protecting child molesters.

Something's very wrong if a church can't squarely face serious moral problems among its leaders.

Our predicament today is pictured very well in the book of Job. Bildad, one of Job's friends, gives this description of someone who forgets God: "He leans on his house, but it does not stand. He holds it fast, but it does not endure. . . . His roots wrap around the rock heap, and look for a place in the stones" (Job 8:15, 17). Roots wrapped around a pile of rocks—that's how many people feel today. What was supposed to be a solid support is just a rock heap.

Solid ground is hard to come by these days. Where can we put our roots down with confidence? If God doesn't seem to be making a real difference in many churches, where do we find Him? Is He really there?

Scandals in the church trouble us. Terror in the name of God troubles us even more.

Today, many individuals in the Middle East claim to have joined a holy war. They strap bombs around themselves, walk into a restaurant, and blow up men, women, and children by the score. And they claim to be devout Muslims.

Today, you have people praising the name of Allah because thousands of civilians were incinerated at the World Trade Center. Is that the difference God makes? Is that what faith and devotion produce? Murderous fanatics are giving religion a bad name. They've gotten the headlines. They make us wonder: Is there a good place left where we can put down our roots of faith?

How do we get through the "heavy stuff"? Does God really make a difference in the world today? Let me show you what I discovered in the nation of Papua New Guinea.

The *It Is Written* telecast ministry sponsored a satellite evangelistic series, originating in Port Moresby's large stadium where 100,000 people attended. Tens of thousands of people made a commitment to Jesus Christ in baptism. And something happened as a result that caught the attention of the nation's newspapers. Major crime decreased dramatically! For months following the meetings, the decrease in crime was noted in various parts of Papua New Guinea. God did make a difference in that country!

I've seen God making a difference all around the world. In my work as an evangelist, I've talked with scores of people from many different cultures. I've heard their stories. Lives are being transformed. It's exciting. It's dramatic. And most important of all, it's personal.

Let me show you exactly what does make a difference. This is how you sink your roots deep and build a strong faith. Jesus laid it out for His disciples very clearly. He says, "I am the vine, you are the branches. He who abides in Me, and I in him, bears much fruit; for without Me you can do nothing" (John 15:5).

How do we human beings "bear much fruit"? That is, how does God make a difference in our lives, how does He produce good results? There's only one way. We have to abide in Christ. We have to become personally connected to Him—the True Vine. We have to sink our roots into Him as Savior and Lord and Friend.

And what happens when we don't maintain this connection? "If anyone does not abide in Me, he is cast out as a branch and is withered" (verse 6). If you don't stay personally connected to Christ, you wither, your spiritual life shrivels up. And you don't produce any fruit.

But the good news is that the True Vine is always there; the connection is always possible.

What made such a dramatic impact in Papua New Guinea was people connecting personally to Jesus Christ. That's what mattered. That's what actually reduced crime in that entire society. People didn't come forward in those meetings to discuss church policy. They weren't just trying to get connected to a religion. They were sinking their roots into a person—Jesus Christ.

Paul tells us exactly what the "fruits" of such a connection with Jesus the Vine will be. He says, "The fruit of the Spirit is love, joy, peace, longsuffering, kindness, goodness, faithfulness, gentleness, self-control" (Galatians 5:22, 23). That, my friends, is the real difference God makes.

He creates love where there was animosity.

He creates joy where there was despair.

He creates peace where there was anxiety.

I've seen it on faces in Papua New Guinea, on faces in Madras, on faces in Bucharest, on faces in London and Los Angeles. God makes that kind of difference. Abiding in Christ makes that kind of difference.

When you're being nourished by that True Vine, the Spirit produces goodness and self-control. People with those qualities don't molest children. They don't abuse their office. The Spirit produces kindness and faithfulness. People with those qualities don't betray a sacred trust.

Sinking your roots into a church is *not* the same as sinking your roots into Jesus. I believe that is the real message of the clergy scandals that have troubled so many people: It's possible to have all the right church connections but to miss out on the one really important connection. It's possible to hold a high church office, and yet wither spiritually.

Clergy who hide crimes under their robes are branches that are cut off; they're disconnected. They're not taking nourishment from the one True Vine that enables human beings to bear fruit. Their roots are wrapped around a pile of rocks.

I believe how a church responds to a crisis tells a lot about where its roots lie. The Roman Catholic Church isn't the only church to be rocked by scandal in recent years. But its response to the problem of pedophilia among priests is instructive. It has a sobering message for all of us concerned about faith.

Many church leaders and lay people have worked very hard to make sure that those who abuse their office are held accountable and are prevented from hurting more people. But many others, when confronted by the scandal, rushed to the defense of church institutions. Their first concern was protecting the priesthood.

One church leader warned about attacks on the "twin towers" of supernatural life. What are those twin towers? According to this leader they are the priesthood and the sacraments. Celibate priests are "Christ among us," he wrote. They have the mystical power to make Him supernaturally present in the sacraments.

It's this kind of response that has made many sincere Catholics question their faith. Molesting children is a horribly destructive thing. It's one of the worst kinds of betrayals we can imagine. And if a church deals with this problem by trying to put its priests on an even higher pedestal—that's pretty scary. That's why many Catholics are outraged. That's what disturbs people of faith from many different backgrounds.

Roman tradition has elevated the celibate priesthood far above the human realm. Priests are supposed to have the supernatural ability to re-create Christ's sacrifice all over again when they administer the sacrament.

Well, guess what? Priests are very human. The church makes mistakes, big mistakes. Church leaders are not perfect.

Institutions are *not* where you want to put down your deepest roots. They're not the firmest foundation. Institutions fail. When scandals erupt, the solution is not to try to prop up the institution. The solution is not to try to put the clergy in a supernatural category. It's not to protect the "twin towers" at all costs.

Institutions fail. But the True Vine remains. That's where we need to sink our faith roots. That's a firm foundation. We need to find a body of believers where that True Vine is honored, where people can build that personal connection, where God is making a difference.

Let me share with you something Christ said about *how* we can abide in the Vine. "If you abide in Me, and My words abide in you, you will ask what you desire, and it shall be done for you" (John 15:7). Abiding in Christ means that Christ's words abide in you. You are studying His words each day, meditating on His words, applying His words, internalizing His words.

Jesus has wonderful things to tell us. He has the Word that will light up our path. He has the Word that will clear up our confusion. He has the Word that will comfort our hearts. He has the Word that will dispel our doubts. He has the Word that will correct our mistakes. He has the Word that will guide us into eternity. Jesus has the Word! Listen to what He told the disciples: "I have called you friends, for all things that I heard from My Father I have made known to you" (John 15:15).

Jesus is our personal connection to all the wisdom of heaven. He's our personal connection to the fullness of God. Yes, there's much good fruit in that one True Vine. But we have to abide in Him, abide in His words.

Do you want strong roots for your faith? Send those roots down deep into the Word of God. Take in the words of Christ. Take them in personally and individually. It's all about communication.

How does God make a difference? It's one-on-one. It's each branch connected to the Vine. It's the words of Christ flowing into our hearts.

Churches can help that process. Or sometimes they can get in the way. Sometimes they can help us understand Christ's words more clearly. Sometimes church traditions just obscure those words.

Where are your roots today?

I believe the time has come for us to sink our roots into something that's truly divine. Sometimes pride in our traditions actually blocks that process. The right ecclesiastical connections aren't enough. Sometimes we don't go deep enough, back to that original Vine, back to the words of Christ Himself, back to the original Source of spiritual nurture, the universal Source of good fruit.

Let's be honest about it. Institutions sometimes get in the way of that all-important connection. As we look at a church, we have to ask ourselves, "Am I finding a personal connection with Christ there? Am I seeing His Word honored there? Am I learning to dig into the riches of Scripture there?"

Friends, ancient traditions aren't good enough. A church with a long legacy isn't good enough. What's become clear today is that we can sink our roots into all that—and still wither spiritually. No religious garments, no titles, no privileges, no supposedly supernatural powers, can make up for a lack of connection.

We need to find a place where *all* of God's Word is honored, where *all* God's eternal commandments are obeyed. Bending the law to suit our customs just won't do. Making exceptions because of someone's position just won't do. Picking and choosing among Christ's principles just won't do.

In this time of scandal and terror, we need to sink our roots into the eternal, unchanging, ever-fruitful, refreshing, renewing Word of God.

We *can* go back to a time of certainty, to a sense of serenity. We *can* return to that home again. It's not as far away as we may imagine, even in a world of suicide bombers and holy war. God *is* making a dramatic difference today. He's doing it one heart at a time. He's doing it through His Word. It's right at our fingertips. A strong, deeply rooted faith is there for the taking.

Will you determine to find it today? If you've lost touch, will you determine to reach out today? If your spirituality has withered, will you determine to establish that connection today? If your faith roots are curling around a pile of rocks, will you determine to sink them deep in the True Vine? Deep into Jesus Christ and His Word?

Make that decision, and you will discover for yourself that God does indeed make all the difference.

How Many Redeemers?

Stanley was getting fed up with crime in the neighborhood. Too many break-ins. Too many prowlers. His suburb just wasn't what it used to be. The city seemed to be getting closer and closer.

So Stanley decided to do something about it. He bought a heavy metal screen to cover his front door. He had steel bars installed outside all the windows. He put dead bolts on all the doors. He wired in a security system that automatically locked everything.

Finally, Stanley felt safe. Nobody was going to break into his castle. But a few weeks later, a fire started in his kitchen while Stanley was taking a nap. Awakened by the smoke, he tried to rush outside, but all the doors were bolted shut; all the windows were barred. Sadly, Stanley wasn't able to disarm all the locks before succumbing to the fire.

In this chapter, we're going to discover how to put down our faith roots in a way that brings us security, even in a very insecure world. Everyone is looking for more security these days. But sometimes the biggest threats aren't outside somewhere. Sometimes they're very close to home. Sometimes our safety depends on finding a way out.

We're all keenly aware of evil in the world today. We realize that people can hate in the name of God. We realize that highly educated human beings can plot to slaughter thousands of innocent people. We realize that people who pray regularly can devote themselves to terror.

We want to imagine that nothing like that could possibly happen here at home. But then we remember Timothy McVay, the young man from America's heartland who seemed so polite and nice—and who chose to blow up hundreds of strangers in Oklahoma City.

Something terrible can happen to the human heart. It's something the prophet Jeremiah described very precisely long ago. "The heart is deceitful above all things, and desperately wicked; who can know it?" (Jeremiah 17:9). People can actually persuade themselves that random acts of terror are part of a holy cause. That is evidence that the heart can be "deceitful above all things."

To really experience security we need to find an answer for the evil in human hearts. We need a solution for the sin problem.

And so people are looking for a faith that gives us that answer. People are looking for a God who can take on human cruelty. People are looking for a Redeemer. We want to be able to sink our faith roots into something that will hold. We need to find a Redeemer we can count on.

So, it's vitally important that we understand just what kind of Redeemer answers this fundamental human need. It's important because sometimes we can sink our faith roots in the wrong thing!

Let me show you the Redeemer whom the writers of the New Testament present to us. Read this wonderful description from the apostle Paul:

> The Father . . . has qualified us to be partakers of the inheritance of the saints in the light. He has delivered us from the power of darkness and translated us into the kingdom of the Son of His love, in whom we have redemption through His blood, the forgiveness of sins. He is the image of the invisible God, the firstborn over all creation (Colossians 1:12-15).

That's what God has accomplished through the Son, Jesus Christ. He has confronted evil head-on.

He can deliver us from the power of darkness.

He can transfer us to the kingdom of "the Son of His love."

We can experience redemption in Christ because He died for sinful humanity. He made forgiveness possible.

Jesus Christ is supremely qualified to be our Redeemer. He's qualified because He is the very image of God, who took on our weaknesses. He's qualified because He is the firstborn over all creation who laid down His life to reconcile all of creation to a holy God. Jesus Christ offers us eternal security. As long as we choose Him, He chooses us. That's why Jesus is qualified to be the Redeemer of the world.

But do you know what has happened down through history? Human beings can't leave well enough alone.

In our endless quest for security we actually try to *add* to the redemption that Christ worked out. We want to make salvation more of a sure thing. Some people have even tried to multiply the Redeemer.

Let me give you one example.

Recently, a movement in the Roman Church has gained quite a bit of momentum. It's a movement to establish Mary, the mother of Jesus, as a co-redeemer of humanity. An organization called "Voice of the People for Mary Mediatrix" collected more than four million signatures. It is claimed that the Virgin Mary suffered at the cross, with her Son, for us all. It is claimed that by her obedience she undid Eve's disobedience. By her faith she undid Eve's disbelief.

Interestingly enough, this has been a Roman doctrine for a long time. What people want now is to elevate belief in Mary as a co-redeemer and co-mediator to the level of dogma, a divinely inspired truth.

Why? Why make Mary another savior? Many people of faith don't get it. Many Catholics themselves are deeply disturbed by it.

To get the bigger picture we have to go back to A.D. 1000. You see, shortly before the close of the first millennium after Christ, believers began to fear He might come again on that date—A.D. 1000. Yes, they "feared" the Second Coming greatly.

Why?

Because many people in the Middle Ages had come to picture Jesus Christ as a stern judge riding down to earth to seek vengeance for thousands of years of sin. He was so perfect, so holy, so lofty. How could sinful human beings possibly approach Him? So they began praying desperately to His mother, Mary: "Please save us from the wrath of the Lamb."

And A.D. 1000 came and went—and the earth didn't end.

Devotion to the Virgin Mary really accelerated after that nonevent. She had rescued the world, it was said. She'd put off the awful judgment. Why do people want to elevate Mary as co-redeemer? Because, to many, she seems more approachable than Jesus. She's a mother, after all. She must have a tender heart.

But guess what? Even Mary can seem a bit removed. After all, Catholic doctrine affirms the Immaculate Conception—the belief that Mary was born without original sin. It affirms her Assumption—the belief that she was taken bodily into heaven at her death.

Mary, as the mother of God, is pictured way up there, almost out of reach. And so many Catholics began to form attachments to various martyrs and saints. They began to pray that these holy individuals might intercede, put in a good word for them with God. It seemed safer approaching a saint.

But still, the saints were dead. They were supposedly up in heaven. So people kept looking for something they could see and touch in order to feel secure. And they tried to find it in their local priest. They came to see him, not just as someone pointing them to the sacrifice of Christ on their behalf. No, that bread and wine he was holding in his hands was magically transformed into the actual body and blood of Christ. That man standing there in front of you could offer atonement; he could offer forgiveness in the confessional.

So, in the end, the search for security multiplied redeemers. If one redeemer is good, two are better. And if two are good, why not have a host of them? Having a lot of redeemers is like having a lot of good places to hide from evil.

But the question is: Do more hiding places mean more safety?

Hiding places multiply when we're afraid, when we're driven by fear. That's the sad fact behind all those redeemers. Redeemers multiply when we're not looking at the right one.

Think about what happened in the religion of many redeemers—the religion of saints and the mediating Virgin Mary. It was a notoriously insecure system. It produced indulgences in the Middle Ages. Indulgences were an attempt to buy your way out of purgatory, a way to ensure you wouldn't drop down to hell. When all else fails, maybe money will help, maybe the right ritual would bring forgiveness.

It produced a religion of merit. Ordinary believers were always trying to earn the pardon that Christ offered. The Roman Church of the medieval period almost lost sight of the great truth of justification by faith. It took the Reformation to bring it to light again.

The church that tried to add to the merits of Christ, subtracted from assurance. The church that multiplied redeemers, divided redemption.

So, what's the bottom line? More redeemers *don't* mean more security. The opposite is true. We need to find the one Redeemer who really does take us to the one place of eternal safety. That is where we need to sink our faith roots.

The writers of the New Testament take pains to give us solid ground for security. Here is wonderful assurance: "God . . . desires all men to be saved and to come to the knowledge of the truth. For there is one God and one Mediator between God and men, the Man Christ Jesus, who gave Himself a ransom for all" (1 Timothy 2:3-6).

God isn't playing games with us. He's not trying to make salvation as difficult to find as possible. No! He wants every human being to come into His place of safety. That's precisely why He's given us one Mediator!

There's only one Jesus Christ. There's only one Savior. There's only one Intercessor. There's only one Redeemer. There's only one High Priest in heaven. There's only one Lord. There's only one Lamb of God who takes away the sin of the world!

There's only one because more redeemers mean less security. There's only one because one is enough. Jesus paid the full price of sin; He laid down His perfect life for us all. His redemption doesn't need anything added. It doesn't need completion. It is finished.

We've got to sink our faith roots in the right place, friends. That's important. We can't keep running from one inadequate hiding place to another. We've got to find security in the righteousness of Christ.

When you bury your faith roots in this Redeemer, security becomes so much simpler, so much easier. The apostle John says, "God has given us eternal life, and this life is in His Son. He who has the Son has life; he who does not have the Son of God does not have life" (1 John 5:11, 12).

Did you catch that? Eternal life is *a gift!* It's not something you earn or deserve. It's not something complicated you have to figure out. It's not a divine payback at the end of some long religious ritual. It's a gift. And that gift is in Jesus Christ. So, if you accept Jesus Christ by faith as your Redeemer, you've got the gift. If you've got the Son, you've got everything.

That's our place of safety in a world scarred by evil and cruelty. That's our place of safety as human beings whose hearts are deceitful. That's our place of safety when every other hiding place fails.

There's one big reason you can find a place of complete safety in the Redeemer, Jesus Christ, even in a world plagued by evil. He defeated our great enemy at the Cross. He defeated the worst that human beings could do to Him. He defeated the vilest cruelty. Paul writes about how Christ made us alive even while we were dead in our sins. And then he pens these words describing the Cross as an act of conquest: "And having disarmed the powers and authorities, he made a public spectacle of them, triumphing over them by the cross" (Colossians 2:15, NIV).

Christ triumphed over evil forces at the Cross. Christ won His great conflict against Satan. Christ disarmed everything that seeks to destroy our souls. That's why the book of Revelation tells us that believers overcome the evil one "by the blood of the Lamb" (Revelation 12:11). Our enemy, the tempter, won't go near that blood. It spells his doom. He is utterly defeated by the Cross.

And so the Cross remains our place of safety. It's our one place of safety—yesterday, today, and forever.

That's the place where we find forgiveness. That's the place where we find peace. That's the place where we begin to experience God's love. That's the place where eternal life starts.

Please remember this—God wants you to have assurance. He wants you to find a place of safety. But you don't find it by multiplying redeemers and multiplying hiding places. You find it by responding to the Savior's wonderful invitation: "If anyone thirsts, let him come to Me and drink. He who believes in Me, as the Scripture has said, out of his heart will flow rivers of living water" (John 7:37, 38).

We all have a deep longing for a place of safety, for a feeling of security. Jesus promises us we can find it. That longing can be satisfied. Just come and drink. It's that simple. Drink freely. Just put your trust in the Mediator and Redeemer. Take in His assurances. You'll find they become a fountain of living water welling up inside you. It's not complicated. It's not something you have to deserve. It's right here, right now. But you have to take the plunge.

Have you found your place of safety yet? Have you been able to sink your faith roots into something secure? I invite you to take a drink from the Water of Life Jesus offers. Just hold out your hands. Get your faith wet. Taste and see that this gift is good. God has gone to great lengths to bring you eternal security through the one Redeemer who can save us to the uttermost.

Won't you take Him up on His offer just now?

Is There a Remnant?

Two concussion bombs fall from the sky over the ancient city of Petra and find their target. A million people have gathered there to listen to a rabbinical scholar, Dr. Ben-Judah, talk about the Messiah. Each explosion creates a fireball 6,000 feet in diameter. The man who sent these bombs, Nicolae Carpathia, an antichrist figure who heads something called the "Global Community," is confident these believers have been incinerated.

Down among the rocks of Petra people are indeed burning alive. But they're not even harmed. In fact, they start dancing and worshiping in the flames. Soon a huge fountain of water erupts out of the ground and puts out the fire.

This is a dramatic scene from the book *The Remnant,* part of the best-selling "Left Behind" ™ * series of novels, which picture events at the end of the world. The book has focused a lot of attention on a group the Bible calls "the remnant." In the novel this group is known as the "Tribulation Force." This underground

*Trademark owned by Tyndale House Publishers, Wheaton Illinois.

movement has infiltrated the antichrist's organization and is busy trying to undermine it. There's a lot of intrigue and disguises and chases and heavy weaponry in the book. But, we're told, it's this group, the remnant, who will be around to celebrate in the end, at the glorious appearing of Jesus Christ.

There's a whole lot of shaking going on in the "Left Behind" ™ series. And there's a whole lot of shaking going on in the world today. Fanatical figures are urging people to unite in a holy war. Terror strikes closer and closer to home. Religious groups are trying to enforce their claims—with the gun.

So where we put down our faith roots matters a lot. People can obviously put down roots in the wrong place, give their allegiance to the wrong religious leaders. How do we know which side we'll be on in the end times? How do we know that today's zeal won't turn into tomorrow's fanaticism?

Just who are the remnant? Does the Bible define that group precisely? Can we know we're a part of it?

In this chapter, you're going to get some clear answers, straight from Scripture. You're going to find out about God's chosen, and how you can avoid becoming attached to the wrong group. More and more people are wanting to put down roots today. They want a home for their hearts. They want a home for their faith. In this chapter, you'll discover what it really means to find yourself among the chosen—the remnant.

Let's start with the apostle Paul. He's writing to the believers in Ephesus, telling them exactly what it means to be the chosen people:

Now, therefore, you are no longer strangers and foreigners, but fellow citizens with the saints and members of the household of God, having been built on the foundation of the apostles and prophets, Jesus Christ Himself being the chief cornerstone, in whom the whole building, being joined together, grows into a holy temple in the Lord, in whom you also are being built together for a habitation of God in the Spirit (Ephesians 2:19-22).

The remnant church is not going to be built on plots and counterplots. It's not going to be built on weapons. It's built on one thing, one cornerstone—Jesus Christ. He's the One who turns foreigners into fellow citizens. He turns strangers into members of the household of God. He's the Chief Cornerstone in a foundation built by apostles and prophets.

With this in mind, let's look at what the apostle John writes about Satan's final persecution of God's people. In the book of Revelation, the church is symbolized by a woman, and believers are represented as her children. John writes:

And the dragon was enraged with the woman, and he went to make war with the rest of her offspring, who keep the commandments of God and have the testimony of Jesus Christ (Revelation 12:17).

"The rest of her offspring." That's the remnant of her offspring, the people of God living in the end time.

And how are they identified? They keep the commandments of God and they have the testimony of Jesus Christ. In other words, they're growing out of the right foundation. They're growing out of the commandments, passed on through the apostles and prophets. They're growing out of all that Jesus said, His testimony. Jesus revealed things about life from God the Father's perspective. He saw the big picture. That's His testimony.

The Father adopts us as His children in Jesus Christ. That's part of His testimony. That's why we belong. The remnant is a group built on that Rock, that Cornerstone. They're putting roots down in the right foundation.

"Well," you might be saying, "aren't all churches built on that foundation?"

Not quite. Churches have a tendency to build up their own tradition and dogma. That's understandable. We all want to organize the truth to some extent. But sometimes we pile up such a mass of interpretation and explanation that we cover up the simple testimony of Jesus. Some churches start paying much more attention to their traditions than to the plain statements of Scripture. They stop building on the Rock. They lose an essential quality of the remnant.

All kinds of churches have done this, but pardon me if I give one specific example.

If you walk into St. Peter's Basilica in Rome today, you will see a huge inscription high up on the walls of the central nave. St. Peter's is quite an inspiring place; it's filled with beautiful works of art to the glory of God. And there, going around the nave, are words in Latin taken from a New Testament text in Matthew 16: "On this rock I will build My church" (verse 18).

Now, there have been centuries of debate, between Catholics and Protestants, about what Jesus meant by the words, "this rock." Roman Catholics have placed a great deal of weight on this text. That's why it's inscribed in St. Peter's Basilica. Catholics have taken "this rock" to mean Peter. In Greek, Peter, or *petros,* means "rock." Catholics say Jesus founded His church on Peter and gave him special authority, the keys to the kingdom.

As a result, Catholics have felt that church tradition carries a lot of authority. What the popes officially teach, as the successors of Peter, is assumed to be divine truth.

Most Protestants would argue that in the New Testament Peter never seems to assume any special authority over the other apostles. Some argue that the Greek word *petros* means a small pebble—not a rock that could serve as a foundation for a church.

But here's what I think is the real issue. Let's assume that Peter *was* the first leader of the early church. Let's assume that Christ gave him special authority. Does that make Peter higher than Christ? Does that give what Peter says more weight than the "testimony of Jesus"? Of course not. Peter didn't give Jesus authority; it was the other way around. Jesus gave Peter authority.

Jesus is the Cornerstone. Period. Jesus is the Rock from which everything else grows. The successors of Peter don't have more authority than Jesus. Church councils don't have more authority than Jesus. That's what many people are realizing today—both Catholics and non-Catholics.

Such ideas as purgatory and the Virgin Mary's Immaculate Conception and confession to priests are definitely not part of the "testimony of Jesus." They're not supported in the Bible. Church tradition, however, has turned them into dogma. It has superseded Scripture.

I find something very ironic in those Latin words inscribed up there in St. Peter's Basilica. The Church of Rome has based its great authority on the Scripture: "On this rock I will build My church."

But think about it. That's using Scripture to show you're above Scripture! That's appealing to the authority of the Word to prove you can overrule the Word!

Well, it's easy to point out this Catholic inconsistency. But all of us—all people of faith—must beware of building on any other foundation than the "testimony of Jesus." We've got to build directly on that Cornerstone. That's the first essential mark of the remnant. That's where you can put down your faith roots.

Now, let's look at another essential mark. Listen to what the apostle Peter himself had to say about Jesus Christ as the Chief Cornerstone: "Therefore, to you who believe, He is precious; but to those who are disobedient . . . 'a stone of stumbling and a rock of offense' " (1 Peter 2:7, 8).

That wonderful Cornerstone will become a stumbling block to some. People will trip over the testimony of Jesus. People will find it objectionable. This applies to the group growing directly from that Cornerstone. They're going to be proclaiming truths that make people stumble. They don't just repeat all the popular lines. Their message isn't just something you can accept automatically without thought.

Sometimes what we don't want to hear is the very thing that can free us. Let's look again at the book of Revelation. We see the picture of the remnant as a stumbling block echoed in chapter 14. Here God's last warning message to the world is laid out as something His last-day people will be proclaiming: " 'Babylon is fallen, is fallen, that great city, because she has made all nations drink of the wine of the wrath of her fornication.' . . . 'If anyone worships the beast and his image . . . he himself shall also drink of the wine of the wrath of God' " (Revelation 14:8-10).

In Revelation, Babylon is a symbol of false religious systems. The beast is a figure that persuades people to worship the wrong thing, to put down their roots in the wrong places. And the remnant is warning people that there is danger—"All the world may seem to be worshiping this charismatic figure, but don't go there. It's moral disaster."

And do you know what? Many, many people will stumble right over that message and head on to destruction. It's not what they want to hear.

But the remnant will persevere. They're still firmly grounded in the right foundation. We see them again in verse 12: "Here is the patience of the saints; here are those who keep the commandments of God and the faith of Jesus."

Do you know what "the faith of Jesus" means? It means that sometimes we have to hear what we don't want to hear. Sometimes we have to keep commandments we don't want to keep. Sometimes we have to learn something we don't want to learn. Sometimes we have to realize that the foundation we've been building on is not solid rock at all, but just the creaky scaffolding of tradition. Please forgive me if I step on a few toes now. But maybe we all need our toes stepped on occasionally.

Maybe beautiful liturgy is the heart and soul of your faith. But what happens to those words when you leave the sanctuary? Do they have an impact in your daily life?

Maybe speaking in tongues is your sign that you've got the Holy Spirit. But is He also producing the fruits of love, joy, peace, patience, and self-control?

Maybe you were baptized as an infant, show up at church at Christmas and Easter, and assume you've met the requirements. But are you really ready to meet a Holy God in the last judgment?

Maybe you're just trying to be stricter than your neighbor. But are you aware that legalism is completely incompatible with the everlasting gospel that the remnant proclaim?

Is there something you need to hear? Is there something your church needs to hear?

Please remember: The remnant stands solidly on Jesus Christ. The remnant stands solidly on God's commandments. Practically speaking, they strive to keep all God's commandments. Are there any you're trying to ignore? They keep close to the testimony of Jesus. Is it something you hear only through a filter?

There's one more distinguishing mark of the remnant we can talk about.

The apostle Paul gives us this interesting sidelight on Jesus, the Chief Cornerstone. He pictures Him way back in the time when Israel wandered through the wilderness. He was a Rock for God's people back then, too. Paul says, "And all drank the same spiritual drink. For they drank of that spiritual Rock that followed them, and that Rock was Christ" (1 Corinthians 10:4). Paul is relating Christ to Old Testament pictures of God the Mighty Fortress, the Rock of Refuge. He's also relating Christ to the miracle of water gushing out of a rock to quench the thirst of Israel in the desert.

Jesus has always been a special kind of rock. You can indeed put your roots down deep into this Cornerstone. There's water there. There's nurture there. He provides spiritual drink. And that's something you will always find in the remnant—spiritual nurture, food for the soul. If that's not there, it's not the remnant. Remember, the remnant has the testimony of Jesus. The remnant is being built up on the Cornerstone, the Living Stone that sustains us.

The remnant is a group that nurtures people through the testimony of Jesus, through what he shows us about a heavenly Father's love. The remnant will cause people to stumble. They will speak a prophetic word of warning. But they will always provide spiritual nourishment.

Friends, if you're part of a group that claims to have all the truth, but abuses you—that's not the remnant.

If you're part of a group that drains you—that's not the remnant.

If you're part of a group that dries up your spirit—that's not the remnant.

But there *is* a good place for you today, as there has always been. A place where you belong. I urge you to put down your faith roots in the Cornerstone. Find a place where God's commandments are honored, where following His Word is a high calling. Find a place where the testimony of Jesus occupies center stage. Find a place of nurture. Make an investment of your time there. Make an investment of yourself there. It's a place that I believe your heavenly Father has prepared for you.

* * * * *

Dear Father, thank You that each one of us can become a part of Your remnant, Your chosen ones. Thank You for Jesus Christ, the One who laid Himself down as the Chief Cornerstone. Help us to base our lives in His Word. We want to follow You now, wherever You may want to lead us. Please help us to hear what we don't want to hear. Please show us what we've been ignoring. Please confront us with what we've been avoiding. We pray this because we trust in Your spiritual nurture. Amen.

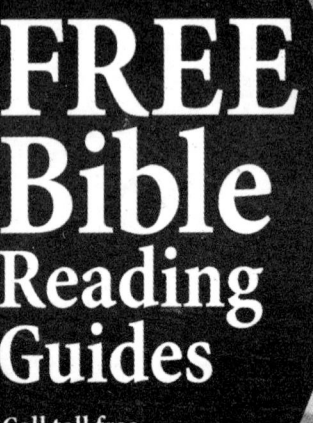
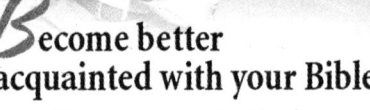